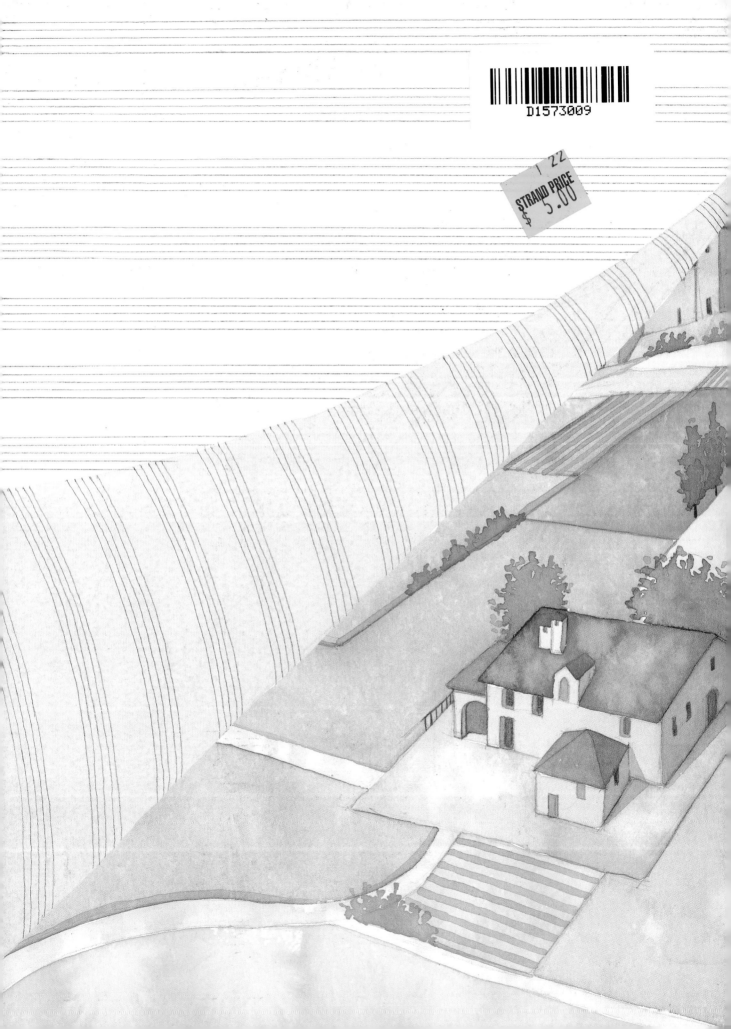

D1573009

The World of Composers

Greta Cencetti

PETER BEDRICK BOOKS

McGraw-Hill
Children's Publishing

A Division of The **McGraw·Hill** Companies

This edition published in the United States in 2002 by
Peter Bedrick Books, an imprint of
McGraw-Hill Children's Publishing,
A Division of The McGraw-Hill Companies
8787 Orion Place
Columbus, Ohio 43240

www.MHkids.com

ISBN 1-58845-473-8

Library of Congress Cataloging-in-Publication Data

Cencetti, Greta.
Verdi / Greta Cencetti.
p. cm. -- (The world of composers)
Summary: An introduction to the life and musical career
of the nineteenth-century Italian composer.
ISBN 1-58845-473-8
1. Verdi, Giuseppe 1813-1901--Juvenile literature. 2. Composers—Italy—
Biography—Juvenile literature. [1. Verdi, Giuseppe 1813-1901.
2. Composers.] I. Title. II. Series.

ML3930.V4 C46 2002
782.1'09--dc21
[B]
2001052537

© 2002 Ta Chien Publishing Co., Ltd.
© 2002 Studio Mouse

10 9 8 7 6 5 4 3 2 1 CHRT 06 05 04 03 02

Printed in China.

The World of Composers

Verdi

Greta Cencetti

PETER BEDRICK BOOKS

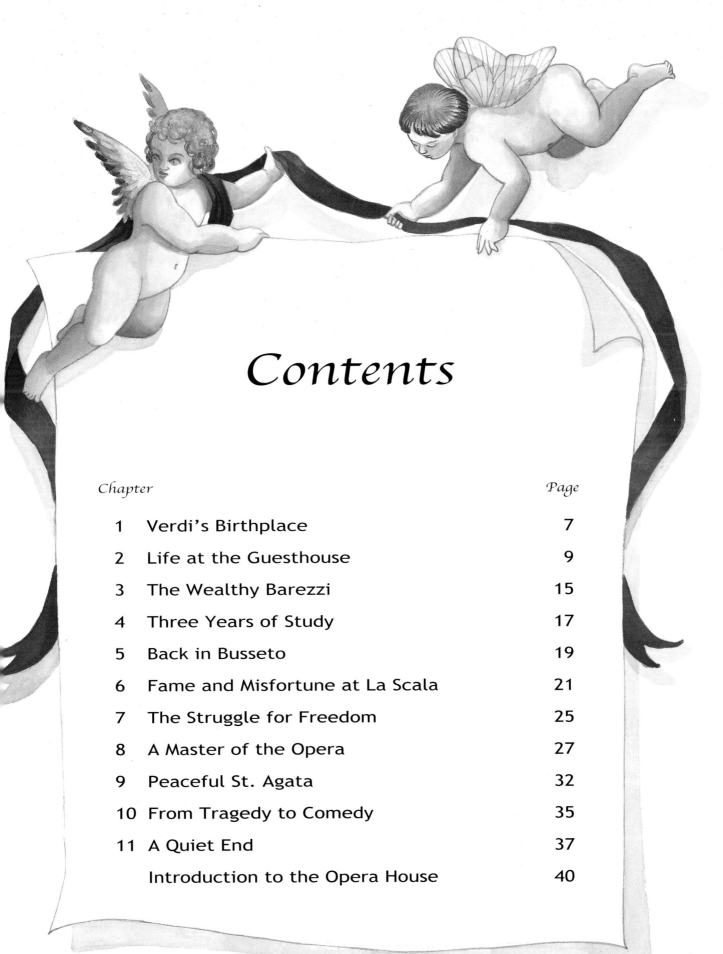

Contents

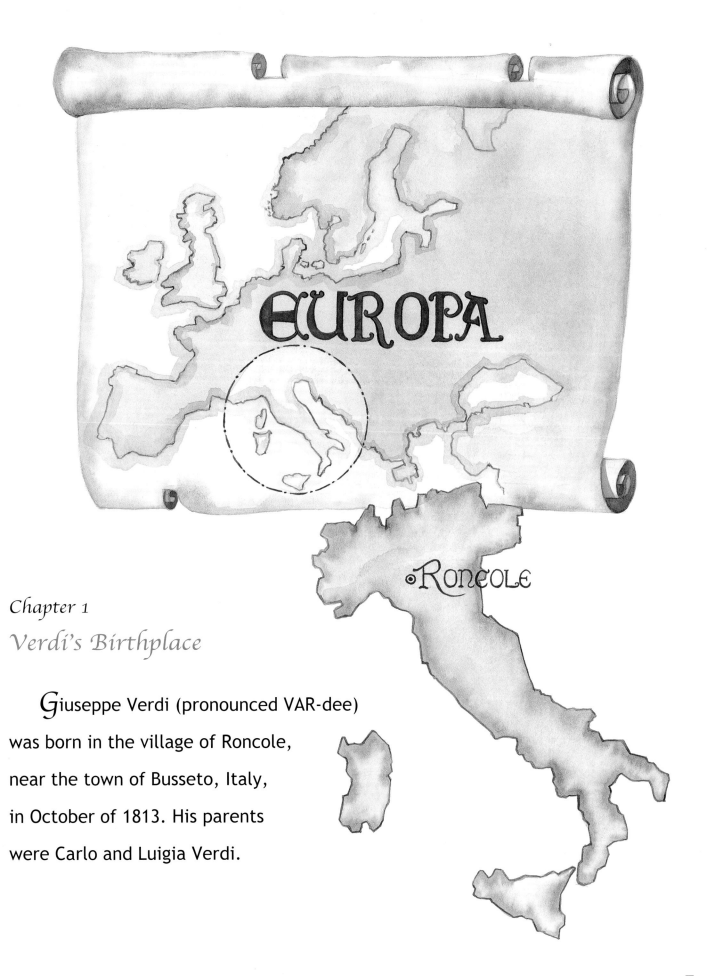

Chapter 1
Verdi's Birthplace

Giuseppe Verdi (pronounced VAR-dee) was born in the village of Roncole, near the town of Busseto, Italy, in October of 1813. His parents were Carlo and Luigia Verdi.

Chapter 2
Life at the Guesthouse

Giuseppe's parents lived in a small house in the village. The Verdis' house was a guesthouse. Verdi's family often took in travelers and other guests, and offered them food and lodging.

Giuseppe's mother and father were known to most of the villagers because of the hospitality they offered their guests. His parents' guesthouse was a favorite spot for local farmers to meet after a long day of work.

Giuseppe has been described as a shy boy, who kept to himself. To escape the busy guesthouse, he would often walk through the countryside or sit by the river, and feed the chickens.

One day, an old violinist came to Roncole and played music to entertain the villagers. In return, Giuseppe's parents offered the violinist a meal at the guesthouse. Young Giuseppe was fascinated by the music of the violin.

Giuseppe's parents soon realized that music came very naturally to their son. They bought him a small piano. Verdi kept this piano for the rest of his life. It reminded him of his love of music as a child and of his kind parents.

The music teacher in the village gave Giuseppe piano lessons and taught him the basics of music. Giuseppe's musical talent amazed the local farmers who heard him play when they attended services in the village chapel. Verdi was an excellent piano student, and, by the age of 12, he was playing the organ for the town church of Busseto.

Chapter 3
The Wealthy Barezzi

*I*n Busseto, there was a wealthy winemaker named Antonio Barezzi. Barezzi loved music, and once in a while he would hear Giuseppe playing the piano in the church near the wine shop.

Sometimes Giuseppe would help Barezzi in the shop, and, in exchange, Barezzi would allow the young boy to play the beautiful piano in his dining room. Verdi and his parents were grateful for this opportunity. Barezzi was like a second father to Verdi.

When Verdi was 15, a traveling theater troupe came to Busseto. They were performing *The Barber of Seville*, the well-known opera by Gioacchino Rossini. In order to attract attention, the troupe announced a special pre-performance show. When Verdi heard this, he immediately went home and wrote a musical introduction for the show. The master of the troupe was so impressed that he allowed Verdi to perform it. The young musician was showing promise of becoming a great composer.

Chapter 4

Three Years of Study

A few years later, Verdi went to the music conservatory in Milan to continue his studies. Unfortunately, he was not accepted because he did not pass the required exams. Verdi was shocked and sad. He even thought about giving up music entirely.

Fortunately, his luck changed. A few days later, a famous teacher, Vincenzo Lavigna, accepted Verdi as a student. Vincenzo was a wonderful teacher, who brought out Verdi's musical talents.

Chapter 5
Back in Busseto

*T*hree years later, Verdi returned to Busseto. There, he began teaching music and started earning an income. On May 4, 1836, Verdi married Barrezzi's daughter, Margherita. They lived in a house that Barrezzi gave them, and they had two children.

Verdi composed while he taught music. He became well respected in the community. It was here that Verdi began writing operas.

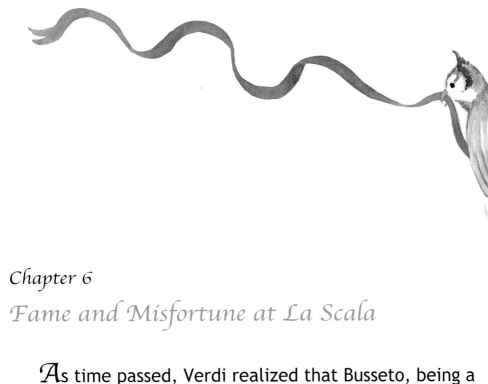

Chapter 6
Fame and Misfortune at La Scala

As time passed, Verdi realized that Busseto, being a small town, did not offer him much chance for growth in his musical career.

In 1838, he decided to move his family to Milan, home of the famous La Scala Theater. People came from around the world to perform at La Scala. It was there that Verdi had the good fortune to meet Merelli, the theater's agent.

Sadly, within two years of arriving in Milan, Verdi's wife and two children died. Although he had begun writing musical works for La Scala, the loss of his family made him so sad that he was unable to continue.

One night, Verdi met with Merelli. Merelli tried to restore the composer's excitement in music. Merelli's encouragement worked, and Verdi was inspired to create the opera, *Nabucco*.

A famous singer, named Giuseppina Strepponi, learned about Verdi's work. She offered to be the principal female vocalist in *Nabucco*. Her performance brought instant success to Verdi. He was invited to perform at the homes of important townspeople.

Verdi's friendship with Giuseppina soon grew into love. They were married on August 29, 1859.

Chapter 7
The Struggle for Freedom

During Verdi's time, Italy was made up of many separate states. Each state had a different ruling noble. None of the states was independent.

It was Verdi's wish for a unified, independent Italy that inspired the opera *Nabucco*. The opera tells the story of how the Jews suffered under the rule of King Nebuchadrezzar of Babylonia.

Chapter 8
A Master of the Opera

Verdi soon became one of the most successful Italian composers. His opera *La Forza del Destino* tells the unhappy love story of Leonora and Don Alvaro. In 1862, Verdi traveled with Giuseppina to St. Petersburg, Russia, to conduct a performance of this opera.

Verdi was popular not only in Italy and Russia, but in Paris too. By now, Verdi was a master of the opera. He was able to compose an opera in only a few hours.

Verdi's most famous operas include *La Traviata* and *Rigoletto*. His operas *Otello*, *Macbeth*, and *Falstaff* were inspired by the works of William Shakespeare. Verdi also composed a few pieces that were not operas, including a *Requiem Mass* (a musical setting of a mass for the dead) in memory of the famous Italian author Alessandro Manzoni.

Another famous opera written by Verdi is called *Aida*. It was first performed in Cairo, Egypt, on December 24, 1871. This opera tells the sad love story of Aida, a girl living in the time when Egypt was under the rule of a Pharaoh. *Aida* has a famous section written for the chorus. This opera made Verdi known around the world.

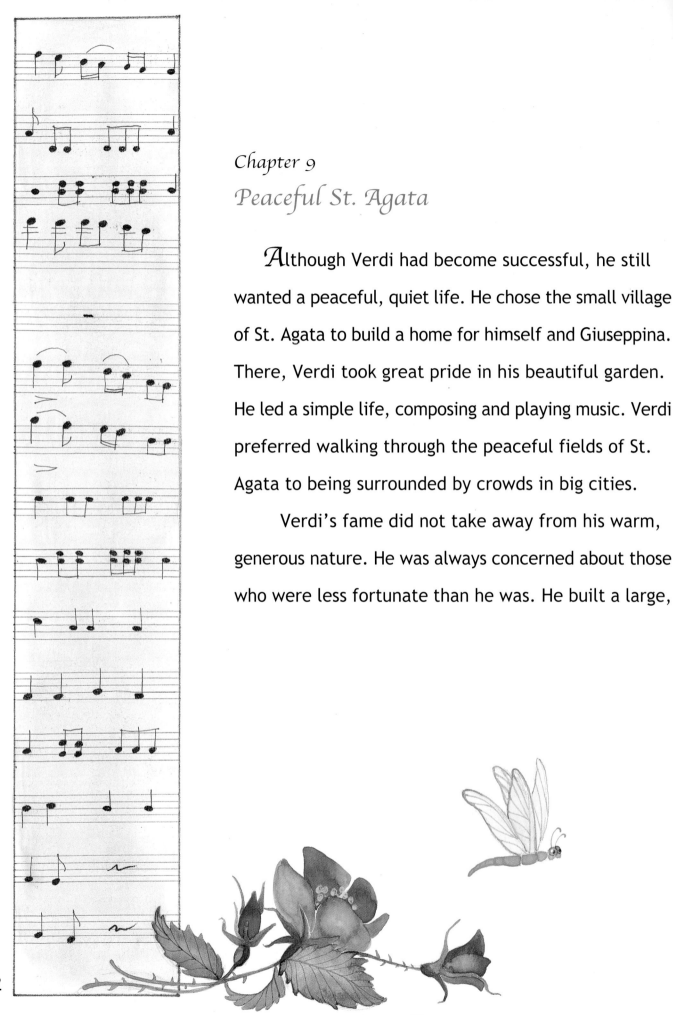

Chapter 9
Peaceful St. Agata

Although Verdi had become successful, he still wanted a peaceful, quiet life. He chose the small village of St. Agata to build a home for himself and Giuseppina. There, Verdi took great pride in his beautiful garden. He led a simple life, composing and playing music. Verdi preferred walking through the peaceful fields of St. Agata to being surrounded by crowds in big cities.

Verdi's fame did not take away from his warm, generous nature. He was always concerned about those who were less fortunate than he was. He built a large,

comfortable home for elderly musicians who were no longer able to earn a living making music. This home, called Casa di Riposo, still exists and is a reminder of Verdi's concern for the well-being of musicians.

By the time Verdi had reached the age of 80, he still looked like a man with great energy and spirit. In old age, he composed less and less, but he never lost his passion for music.

Chapter 10
From Tragedy to Comedy

*T*he last opera that Verdi wrote was *Falstaff*. Before this work, Verdi's operas were always about tragic events. This time, Verdi decided to write about Shakespeare's funny and clever character, Falstaff. This opera was first performed at La Scala on February 9, 1893, and was quite successful.

Chapter 11
A Quiet End

Verdi spent the eight years following the creation of *Falstaff* in St. Agata. His last few years of life were calm and peaceful. In 1901, at the age of 88, Verdi fell ill on the way to Milan.

Giuseppe Verdi passed away on January 27, 1901. His family organized a very simple funeral with no flowers or music, as he had wished. Although Verdi is no longer with us, he lives on as one of the greatest opera composers of all time.

Introduction to the Opera House

Verdi's operas were performed at La Scala, the famous opera house in Milan. Because operas involve acting, singing, and orchestral music, the performance space had special requirements. This led to the construction of a special stage.

The orchestra was located at the front of the stage, but in a lower area called the *orchestra pit*. The conductor would stand on a small, raised platform while directing the orchestra and singers. On the stage, where the singers would perform, was scenery painted on a backdrop known as the *set*. At the front of the stage there was a large curtain. It was raised at the beginning and lowered at the end of each act and, finally, at the end of the performance.

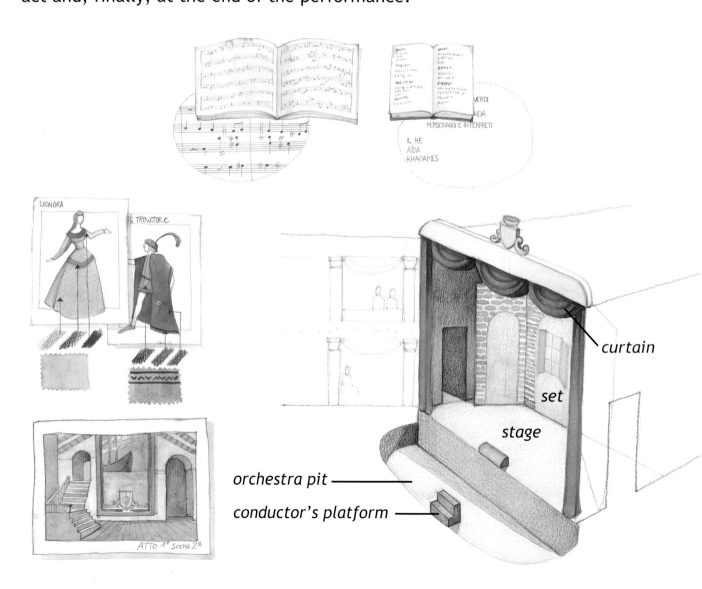

curtain

set

stage

orchestra pit ——

conductor's platform ——

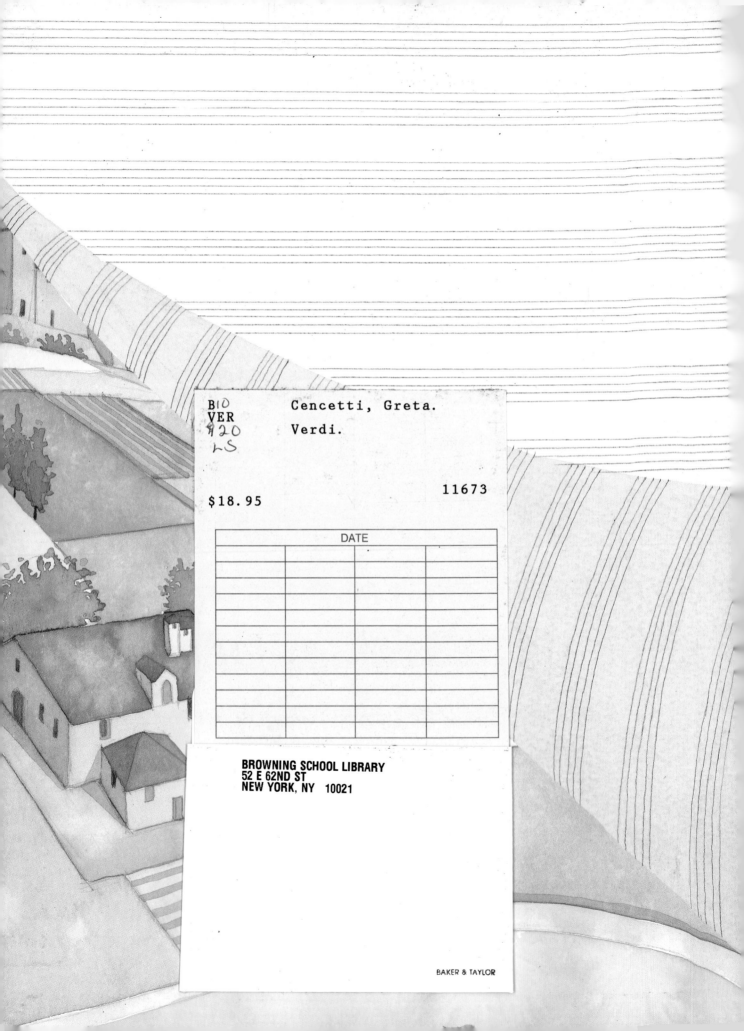